Centurion's Code:

Staying Positive in Policing

Compiled By

David Thornton

Presented To: ______________________

By: ______________________________

Centurion's Code

ISBN 978-1-4357-7264-9

In Locker 32, I built a shrine to the small victories. A collection of photos, thank you notes and a poorly drawn picture in crayon from a victim's child to me was taped to the inside of the locker door. The mementos were there to remind me of the times when I made at least a simple difference in someone's life.

Law enforcement is a tough job that affects people's lives every day. To keep myself focused on service and leaving the scene a little bit better than when I arrived, I began to keep small inspirational quotes to remind me of my responsibilities and to shore me up when I had my doubts.

This book was inspired by a small green booklet that I found behind a file cabinet in Camp Garry Owen Korea. It was a reprint titled "A Warrior's Faith" published probably by an Army Chaplain through an Army printing press. The dedication is to George Bowler Tullidge III, a young sergeant in the 507th Parachute Regiment who died during the D Day assault. His family had collected inspirational quotes in a small notebook. The Tullidges would eventually distribute 300,000 copies to Allied soldiers.

"A Warrior's Faith" added much to my career. I've compiled inspirational quotes and documents gathered over my career into this booklet. Although intended for a law enforcement reader, the intention is the same as the little green book's- *"to give hope and strength."*

Be safe…..

David Thornton
December 24, 2010

It is not the critic who counts; not the man who points out how the strong man stumbles, or where the doer of deeds could have done them better. The credit belongs to the man who is actually in the arena, whose face is marred by dust and sweat and blood; who strives valiantly; who errs, who comes short again and again, because there is no effort without error and shortcoming; but who does actually strive to do the deeds; who knows great enthusiasms, the great devotions; who spends himself in a worthy cause; who at the best knows in the end the triumph of high achievement, and who at the worst, if he fails, at least fails while daring greatly, so that his place shall never be with those cold and timid souls who neither know victory nor defeat.

Theodore Roosevelt

Positive thinking will let you use the abilities, training and experience you have.
Zig Ziglar

Get action. Seize the moment. Man was never intended to become an oyster.
Theodore Roosevelt

Success is not final, failure is not fatal: it is the courage to continue that counts.
Winston Churchill

And now, this is the sweetest and most glorious day that ever my eyes did see.
Donald Cargill

Belief creates the actual fact.
William James

It is during our darkest moments that we must focus to see the light.
Aristotle Onassis

Positive thinking won't let you do anything but it will
let you do everything better than negative thinking will.
Zig Ziglar

A faith is a necessity to a man. Woe to him who believes in nothing.
Victor Hugo

Justice is the firm and continuous desire to render to everyone that which his due.
Justinian

Every obnoxious act is a cry for help.
Zig Ziglar

Tackle the work just in front of you. Strive in an honest way to do the best you can and if, having done your best, there seems to appear the hand of some over-ruling Power which hammers you, take it like a good piece of steel and come right off the anvil with a better temper and a keener edge.
C. W. Post

Hold on with a bulldog grip, and chew and choke as much as possible.
Abraham Lincoln

Never, never, never give up.
Winston Churchill

One man with courage makes a majority.
Andrew Jackson

He who is firm in will molds the world to himself.
Goethe

Forgive many things in others; nothing in yourself.
Ausonius

There is timing in everything.
Miyamoto Mushashi

You cannot tailor make the situations in life, but you can tailor make the attitudes to fit those situations before they arise.
Zig Ziglar

Lack of direction, not lack of time, is the problem.
Zig Ziglar

It takes courage to grow up and become who you really are.
E.E. Cummings

Success is coming up to the level of our best.
Unknown

- Fill your mind with thoughts of peace, courage, hope and health.
- Never try to get even with your enemies.
- Expect ingratitude.
- Count your blessings.
- Try not to imitate others.
- Create happiness for others.

Dale Carnegie

Face your deficiencies and acknowledge them; but do not let them master you. Let them teach you patience, a sweetness, insight…When we do the best we can, we never know what miracle is wrought in our life, or in the life of another.

Helen Keller

We should be too big to take offense and too noble to give it.

Abraham Lincoln

How do you tackle your work each day? With confidence clear or dread?
What to yourself do you stop and say when a new task lies ahead?
What is the thought that is in your mind? Is fear ever running through it?
If so, just tackle the next you find, by thinking you're going to do it.
Edgar Guest

You have to accept whatever comes and the only important thing is that you meet it with courage and with the best that you have to give.
Eleanor Roosevelt

You don't drown by falling in water;
you only drown if you stay there.
Zig Ziglar

We are always on the anvil; by trials God is shaping us for higher things.
Henry Ward Beecher

A man is tomorrow what he thinks today.
Emerson

Be not simply good, be good for something.
Thoreau

The world makes way for a determined man.
Unknown

Failure is an event, not a person.
Yesterday ended last night.
Zig Ziglar

Who bravely dares must sometimes risk a fall.
Thomas Smellett

If thou canst believe, all things are possible to him that believeth.
Mark 9:23

1. Do not think dishonestly.
2. The way is in Training.
3. Become acquainted with every art.
4. Know the ways of all professions.
5. Distinguish between gain and loss in worldly matters.
6. Develop intuitive judgement and understanding for everything.
7. Perceive those things which cannot be seen.
8. Pay attention, even to trifles.
9. Do nothing which is of no use.

Miyamoto Mushashi

A man does what he must - in spite of personal consequences, in spite of obstacles and dangers and pressures - and that is the basis of all human morality.
Winston Churchill

When you are quite content to bear what God has laid upon you, He will soon remove it or show you that it is a real blessing to you.
Unknown

No man is justified in doing evil on the ground of expedience.
Theodore Roosevelt

A ship in the harbor is safe, but that's not what ships are built for.
John Shedd
No man is above the law and no man is below it: nor do we ask any man's permission when we ask him to obey it.
Theodore Roosevelt

Most of us can, if we choose, make this world a palace or a prison.
Lord Avebury

By your own thoughts you make or mar your life, your world, your universe.
Allen

Perfect courage is to do without witnesses what one would be capable of doing with the world looking on.
Francois de La Rochefoucauld

Love life. Be grateful for it always. And show your gratitude by not shying away from its challenges. Always try to live a little beyond your capacities- and you'll find your capabilities are greater than you ever dreamed.
Arthur Gordon

Fear is a terrible companion. It poisons every joy, and takes away the pleasure of any possession. One who lets fear and worry dominate his life can never come within sight of happiness. Faith in God and trust in His protecting love will cast out fear and bring courage and joy.
Unknown

If we had only fair weather, we should never learn how to sail the boat.
Unknown

And let us not be weary in well doing; for in due season we shall reap if we faint not.
Galatians 6:9

Not for a single day
Can I discern the way; But this I know-
Who gives the day will show the way-
So I securely go.
John Oxenham

Life means not submission to but mastery of environment.
Unknown

When we are dealing with people, let us remember we are not dealing with creatures of logic. We are dealing with creatures of emotion, creatures bustling with prejudices and motivated by pride and vanity.
Dale Carnegie

Regardless of your past, tomorrow is a clean slate.
Zig Ziglar

In doing your work in the great world, it is a safe plan to follow a rule I once heard preached on the football field: "Don't flinch; Don't fall; Hit the line hard."
Theodore Roosevelt

I will study and prepare myself and the someday my chance will come.
Abraham Lincoln

- Accept challenge and pain.
- Be close to people.
- Know that you have made a difference.
- Live until you die.

Harold S Kushner

Success in life is a matter not so much of talent or opportunity as of perseverance.
CW Windle

When we have learned to control our thoughts, our sympathies and our emotions, it will be an easy matter to control our circumstances.
Unknown

Be strong and of good courage; be not afraid, neither be thou dismayed: for the Lord the God is with thee whithersoever thou goest.
Joshua 1:9

The quality of a person's life is in direct proportion
to his or her commitment to excellence; regardless of his or her chosen field of endeavor.
Zig Ziglar

Live up to the best that is within you.
Longfellow

People are just as happy as they make up their minds to be.
Abraham Lincoln

They never fail-
Who keep faith with themselves.
Who always give their very best.
Who rise to the attack after falling.
Who maintain their own sense of self respect.
Who return goodwill to the world about them.
Who keep their faith in truth and right unsullied.
Who learn to laugh at difficulties?
Unknown

Desire not to live long, but to live well. How long we live, not years, actions tell.
Watkins

What you do off the job is the determining factor in how far you will go on the job. You build a successful career, regardless of your field of endeavor, by the dozens of little things you do on and off the job.
Zig Ziglar

Heroism is simple, and yet it is rare. Everyone who does the best he can is a hero.
Josh Billings

The lives of true heroism are those in which there are no great deeds to look back upon. It is little things well done in life that go to make a successful and truly good life.
Theodore Roosevelt

Character gets you out of bed; commitment moves you to action. Faith, hope, and discipline enable you to follow through to completion.
Zig Ziglar

Many men owe the grandeur of their lives to their tremendous difficulties.
Spurgeon

Our greatest glory is not in ever falling but in rising every time we fall.
Unknown

With integrity you have nothing to fear since you have nothing to hide. With integrity you will do the right thing, so you will have no guilt. With fear and guilt removed you are free to be and do your best.
Zig Ziglar

Let's have faith that right makes might; and in that faith let us, to the end, dare to do our duty as we understand it.
Abraham Lincoln

What comes out of your mouth is determined by what goes into your mind.
Zig Ziglar

As a tale, so is life; not how long it is but how good it is, is what matters.
Seneca

Let me not pray to be sheltered from dangers but fearless in facing them.

Let me not beg for the stilling of my pain but for the heart to conquer it.

Let me not crave in anxious fear to be saved but hope for the patience to win my freedom.

Grant me that I may not be a coward, feeling your mercy in my success alone; but let me find the grasp of your hand in my failure.
Unknown

Hard things are put in our way, not to stop us, but to call out our courage and strength.
Unknown

It makes a difference to all eternity whether we do right or wrong today.
James F. Clark

Some people find fault like there is a reward for it.
Zig Ziglar

Do your best loyally and cheerfully and suffer yourself to feel no fear nor anxiety. Your times are in God's hands. He has assigned you your place; He will direct your paths; He will accept your efforts if they are faithful.
Canon Farbar

Life is an adventure in forgiveness.
Norman Cousins

I expect to pass through this world but once. Any good thing, therefore, that I can do or any kindness I can show to any fellow human being, let me do it now. Let me not defer nor neglect it, for I shall not pass this way again.
Stephen Grellet

Each day I pray, God give me strength anew.
To do the task I do not wish to do.
To yield obedience, not asking why.
To love and own the truth and scorn the lie.
To look a cold world bravely in the face.
To cheer for those that pass me in the race.
To bear my burdens gaily, unafraid.
To lend a hand to those that need my aid.
To measure what I am by what I give.
God give me strength that I might rightly live!
Unknown

Sometimes you have to let go to see if there was anything worth holding on to.
Unknown

We are what we think.
All that we are arises with our thoughts.
With our thoughts, we make our world.
Buddha

Worry is a futile thing, it's somewhat like a rocking chair,
Although it keeps you occupied, it doesn't get you anywhere.
Anonymous

Life isn't as serious as the mind makes it out to be.

Eckhart Tolle

Life is a shipwreck but we must not forget to sing in the lifeboats.

Voltaire

Law Enforcement Code of Ethics

As a Law Enforcement Officer, my fundamental duty is to serve mankind; to safeguard lives and property; to protect the innocent against deception, the weak against oppression or intimidation, and the peaceful against violence or disorder; and to respect the Constitutional rights of all persons to liberty, equality and justice.

I will keep my private life unsullied as an example to all; maintain courageous calm in the face of danger, scorn or ridicule; develop self-restraint; and be constantly mindful of the welfare of others. Honest in thought and deed in both my personal and official life, I will be exemplary in obeying the laws of the land and the regulations of my department. Whatever I see or hear of a confidential nature or that is confided to me in my official capacity will be kept ever secret unless revelation is necessary in the performance of my duty.

I will never act officiously or permit personal feelings, prejudices, animosities or friendships to influence my decisions. With no compromise for crime and with relentless prosecution of criminal, I will enforce the law courteously and appropriately without fear or favor, malice or ill will, never employing unnecessary force or violence and never accepting gratuities.

I recognize the badge of my office as a symbol of public faith, and I accept it as a public trust to be held so long as I am true to the ethics of the police service. I will constantly strive to achieve these objectives and ideals, dedicating myself before God to my chosen profession...law enforcement.

CANONS OF POLICE ETHICS

Article 1. Primary Responsibility of Job
The primary responsibility of the police service, and of the individual officer, is the protection of the people of the United States through the upholding of their laws; chief among these is the Constitution of the United States and its amendments. The law enforcement officer always represents the whole of the community and its legally expressed will and is never the arm of any political party or clique.

Article 2. Limitations of Authority
The first duty of a law enforcement officer, as upholder of the law, is to know its bounds upon him in enforcing it. Because he represents the legal will of the community, be it local, state or federal, he must be aware of the limitations and proscriptions which the people, through law have placed upon him. He must recognize the genius of the American system of government which gives to no man, groups of men, or institution, absolute power, and he must insure that he, as a prime defender of that system, does not pervert its character.

Article 3. Duty to Be Familiar with the Law and with Responsibilities of Self and Other Public Officials

The law enforcement officer shall assiduously apply himself to the study of the principles of the laws which he is sworn to uphold. He win make certain of his responsibilities in the particulars of their enforcement, seeking aid from his superiors in matters of technicality or principle when these are not clear to him; he will make special effort to fully understand his relationship to other public officials, including other law enforcement agencies, particularly on matters of jurisdiction, both geographically and substantively.

Article 4. Utilization of Proper Means to Gain Proper Ends

The law enforcement officer shall be mindful of his responsibility to pay strict heed to the selection of means in discharging, the duties of his office. Violations of law or disregard for public safety and property on the part of an officer are intrinsically wrong; they are self-defeating in that they instill in the public mind a like disposition. The employment of illegal means, no matter how worthy the end, is certain to encourage disrespect for the law and its officers. If the law is to be honored, it must first be honored by those who enforce it.

Article 5. Cooperation with Public Officials in the Discharge of Their Authorized Duties
The law enforcement officer shall cooperate fully with other public officials in the discharge of authorized duties, regardless of party affiliation or personal prejudice. He shall be meticulous, however, in assuring himself of the propriety, under the law, of such actions and shall guard against the use of his office or person, whether knowingly or unknowingly, in any improper or illegal action. In any situation open to question, he shall seek authority from his superior officer, giving him a full report of the proposed service or action.

Article 6. Private Conduct
The law enforcement officer shall be mindful of his special identification by the public as an upholder of the law. Laxity of conduct or manner in private life, expressing either disrespect for the law or seeking to gain special privilege, cannot but reflect upon the

police officer and the police service. The community and the service require that the law enforcement officer lead the life of a decent and honorable man. Following the career of a policeman gives no man special perquisites. It does give the satisfaction and pride of following and furthering an unbroken tradition of safeguarding the American republic. The officer who reflects upon this tradition will not degrade it. Rather, he will so conduct his private life that the public will regard him as an example of stability, fidelity, and morality.

Article 7. Conduct toward the Public
The law enforcement officer, mindful of his responsibility to the whole community, shall deal with individuals of the community in a manner calculated to instill respect for its laws and its police service. The law enforcement officer shall conduct his official life in a manner such as will inspire confidence and trust. Thus, he will be neither overbearing nor subservient, as no individual citizen has an obligation to stand in awe of him nor a right to command him. The officer will give service where he can, and require compliance with the law. He will do neither from personal

preference or prejudice but rather as a duly appointed officer of the law discharging his sworn obligation.

Article 8. Conduct in Arresting and Dealing with Law Violators
The law enforcement officer shall use his powers of arrest strictly in accordance with the law and with due regard to the rights of the citizen concerned. His office gives him no right to prosecute the violator nor to mete out punishment for the offense. He shall, at all times, have a clear appreciation of his responsibilities and limitations regarding detention of the violator; he shall conduct himself in such a manner as will minimize the possibility of having to use force. To this end he shall cultivate a dedication to the service of the people and the equitable upholding of their laws whether in the handling of law violators or in dealing with the law-abiding.

Article 9. Gifts and Favors
The law enforcement officer, representing government, bears the heavy responsibility of maintaining, in his own conduct, the honor and integrity of all government institutions.

He shall, therefore, guard against placing himself in a position in which any person can expect special consideration or in which the public can reasonably assume that special consideration is being given. Thus, he should be firm in refusing gifts, favors, or gratuities, large or small, which can, in the public mind, be interpreted as capable of influencing his judgment in the discharge of his duties.

Article 10. Presentation of Evidence

The law enforcement officer shall be concerned equally in the prosecution of the wrong-doer and the defense of the innocent. He shall ascertain what constitutes evidence and shall present such evidence impartially and without malice. In so doing, he will ignore social, political, and all other distinctions among the persons involved, strengthening the tradition of the reliability and integrity of an officer's word.

The law enforcement officer shall take special pains to increase his perception and skill of observation, mindful that in many situations his is the sole impartial testimony to the facts of a case.

Article 11. Attitude toward Profession
The law enforcement officer shall regard the discharge of his duties as a public trust and recognize his responsibility as a public servant. By diligent study and sincere attention to self-improvement he shall strive to make the best possible application of science to the solution of crime and, in the field of human relationships, strive for effective leadership and public influence in matters affecting public safety. He shall appreciate the importance and responsibility of his office, and hold police work to be an honorable profession rendering valuable service to his community and his country.

The Bill of Rights

- First Amendment
 Congress shall make no law respecting an establishment of religion, or prohibiting the free exercise thereof; or abridging the freedom of speech, or of the press; or the right of the people peaceably to assemble, and to petition the Government for a redress of grievances.
- Second Amendment .

  A well regulated Militia being necessary to the security of a free State, the right of the people to keep and bear arms shall not be infringed. [5]
- Third Amendment
  No Soldier shall, in time of peace be quartered in any house, without the consent of the Owner, nor in time of war, but in a manner to be prescribed by law.
- Fourth Amendment
  The right of the people to be secure in their persons, houses, papers, and effects, against unreasonable searches

and seizures, shall not be violated, and no Warrants shall issue, but upon probable cause, supported by Oath or affirmation, and particularly describing the place to be searched, and the persons or things to be seized.

- Fifth Amendment
  No person shall be held to answer for any capital, or otherwise infamous crime, unless on a presentment or indictment of a Grand Jury, except in cases arising in the land or naval forces, or in the Militia, when in actual service in time of War or public danger; nor shall any person be subject for the same offence to be twice put in jeopardy of life or limb; nor shall be compelled in any criminal case to be a witness against himself, nor be deprived of life, liberty, or property, without due process of law; nor shall private property be taken for public use, without just compensation.
- Sixth Amendment
  In all criminal prosecutions, the accused shall enjoy the right to a speedy and public trial, by an impartial

jury of the State and district where in the crime shall have been committed, which district shall have been previously ascertained by law, and to be informed of the nature and cause of the accusation; to be confronted with the witnesses against him; to have compulsory process for obtaining witnesses in his favor, and to have the Assistance of Counsel for his defense.

- Seventh Amendment
  In suits at common law, where the value in controversy shall exceed twenty dollars, the right of trial by jury shall be preserved, and no fact tried by a jury, shall be otherwise re-examined in any court of the United States, than according to the rules of the common law.

- Eighth Amendment
  Excessive bail shall not be required, nor excessive fines imposed, nor cruel and unusual punishments inflicted.

- Ninth Amendment
  The enumeration in the Constitution, of certain rights, shall not be

construed to deny or disparage others retained by the people.

- Tenth Amendment
  The powers not delegated to the United States by the Constitution, nor prohibited by it to the States, are reserved to the States respectively, or to the people.

Personal Notes and Messages

Personal Notes and Messages

Personal Notes and Messages

Personal Notes and Messages

www.ingramcontent.com/pod-product-compliance
Ingram Content Group UK Ltd.
Pitfield, Milton Keynes, MK11 3LW, UK
UKHW020215250726
13967UKWH00001B/7

9 781435 772649